SPIN!

Grammar, Vocabulary, and Writing

A

Genevieve J. Kocienda

Longman

Spin! A

Pearson Education, 10 Bank Street, White Plains, NY 10606

Vice president, director of publishing: Allen Ascher
Executive editor: Anne Stribling
Senior development editor: Virginia Bernard
Vice president, director of design and production: Rhea Banker
Executive managing editor: Linda Moser
Production manager: Liza Pleva
Production editor: Sylvia Dare
Director of manufacturing: Patrice Fraccio
Senior manufacturing buyer: Edith Pullman
Cover design: Elizabeth Carlson
Cover art: Mary Jane Begin
Cover photo: © Paul Eekhoff/Masterfile
Text design: Patricia Woszyk
Text composition: TSI Graphics
Text art: Ellen Appleby

ISBN: 0-13-041981-8

1 2 3 4 5 6 7 8 9 10—WC—07 06 05 04 03 02

LONGMAN ON THE WEB

Longman.com offers classroom activities, teaching tips, and online
resources for teachers of all levels and students of all ages. Visit us for
course-specific Companion Websites, our comprehensive online catalogue
of all Longman titles, and access to all local Longman websites, offices,
and contacts around the world.

Join a global community of teachers and students at **Longman.com**.

Longman English Success offers online courses to give learners flexible,
self-paced study options. Developed for distance learning or to complement
classroom instruction, courses cover general English , business English ,
and exam preparation .

For more information visit **EnglishSuccess.com**.

Contents

The Alphabet

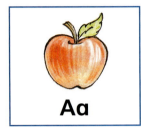 **Aa**

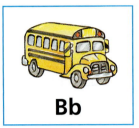 **Bb**

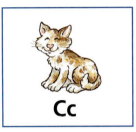 **Cc**

 Dd

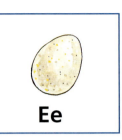 **Ee**

 **Ff**

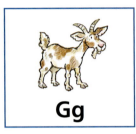 **Gg**

 **Hh**

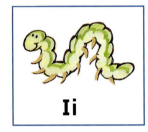 **Ii**

 **Jj**

 **Kk**

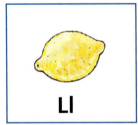 **Ll**

 **Mm**

 **Nn**

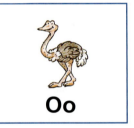 **Oo**

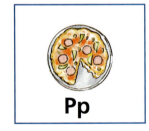 **Pp**

 **Qq**

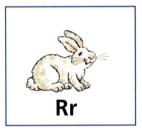 **Rr**

 **Ss**

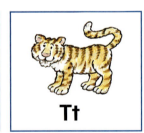 **Tt**

 **Uu**

 **Vv**

 **Ww**

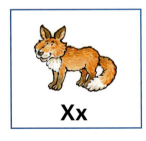 **Xx**

 **Yy**

 **Zz**

Numbers

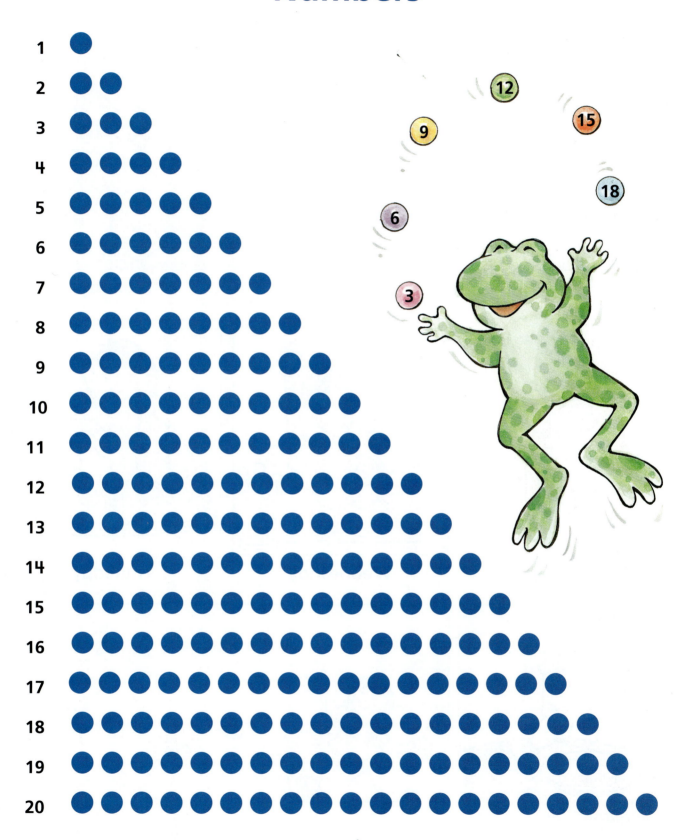

Days of the Week

S	M	T	W	Th	F	S
X						

Sunday

Monday

Tuesday

Wednesday

Thursday

Friday

Saturday

Months of the Year

January	February	March	April

May	June	July	August

September	October	November	December

Colors

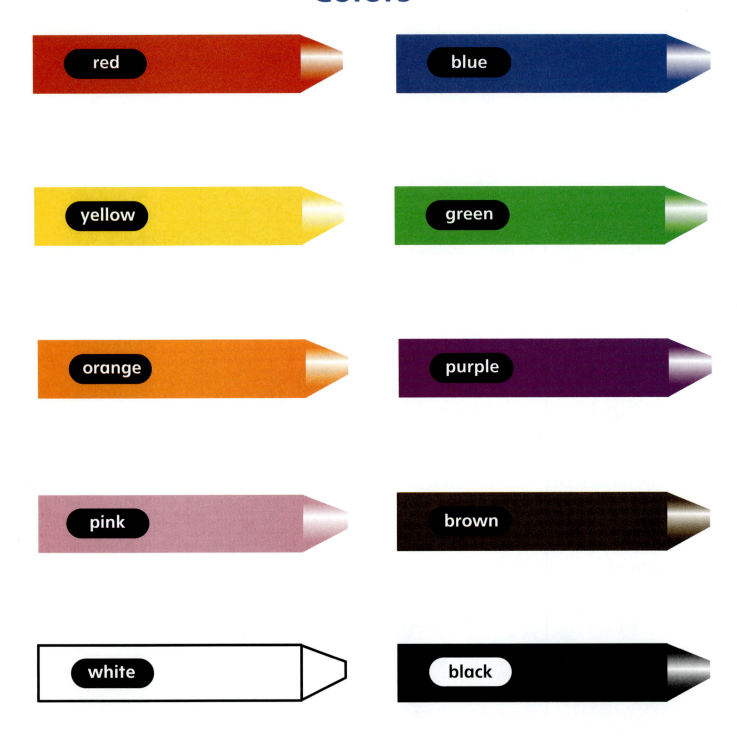

red

blue

yellow

green

orange

purple

pink

brown

white

black

Hello!

In the Classroom

Nouns

A **noun** is a person, place, or thing.

Person	Place	Thing

student	classroom	desk

Point and write.

1. place

classroom

2. thing

desk

3. person

student

Look and write.

teacher

boy

school

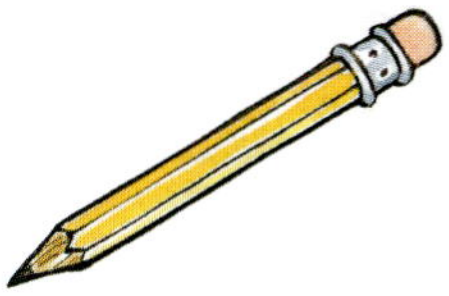

pencil

playground

umbrella

classroom

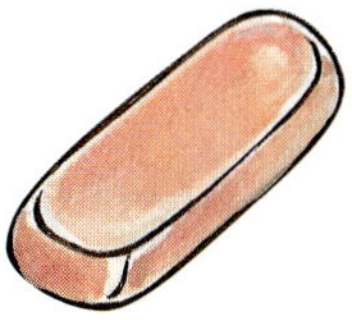

eraser

girl

Person	Place	Thing
teacher		

A/An

Use **a** with words that begin with a consonant.
Use **an** with words that begin with a vowel.

a book

an apple

a school

an umbrella

Point and write.

1.

a teacher

2.

a student

3.

an apple

Look and circle.

1. a / (an) apple

2. a / an book

3. a / an classroom

4. a / an eraser

5. a / an umbrella

6. a / an teacher

7. a / an pencil

8. a / an desk

I am

I am a girl.

I am a boy.

Write and match.

1.

I am a student.

2.

I am a boy.

3.

I am a girl.

4.

I am a teacher.

Draw.

Person

Thing

Place

What is it?

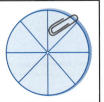

Drop a paper clip onto an object in the circle.

My Family

grandmother

grandfather

father

mother

sister

me

brother

He is/She is

He is a grandfather.

She is a sister.

Point and write.

1.

He is a brother.

2.

She is a mother.

3.

He is a father.

4.

She is a grandmother.

My

My shows belonging.

He is **my** brother.

She is **my** sister.

Draw.

My Family

Circle and write.

My family.

1.

He is my brother.

(brother)   mother

2.

She is my _____.

grandmother   father

3.

He is my _____.

sister   father

4.

She is my _____.

brother   sister

5.

He is my _____.

grandfather   mother

Who is he/she?

Write.

1.

Who is he?
He is my father.

2.

Who is she?
She is my mother.

3.

Who is he?
He is my grandfather.

Write and match.

1.
Who is he?
He is my father.

2.
_____ is she?
She is _____ sister.

3.
_____ is he?
He _____ brother.

4.
_____ is she?
She _____ mother.

5.
_____ is he?
_____ grandfather.

Chant.

Who is he?
He's my brother.
Yes, he is.
Yes, he is.

Who is she?
She's my sister.
Yes, she is.
Yes, she is.

Who is he?
He's my father.
Yes, he is.
Yes, he is.

Who is she?
She's my mother.
Yes, she is.
Yes, she is.

He's = He is
She's = She is

Review: Units 1 and 2

Vocabulary

🎧 **A. Listen and check.**

Nouns

🎧 **B. Listen and check.**

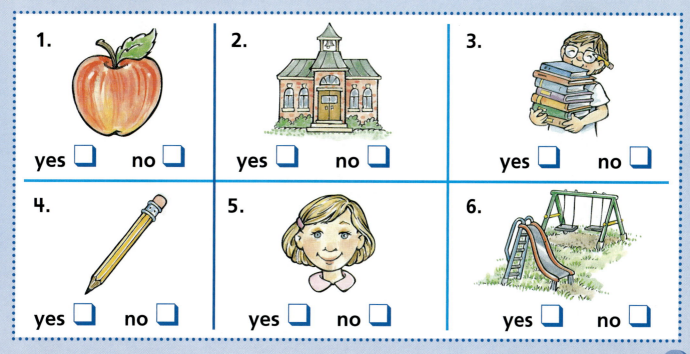

Review: Units 1 and 2

He is/She is

1.
2.
3.

4.
5.
6.

 D. Listen, point, and say.

1.
mother

2.
sister

3.
brother

4.
grandfather

5.
teacher

6.
father

My Body

eye
ear
arm
leg
foot
nose
hand
mouth
feet

My Body

What is it?

What is it?

It is an eye.

What is it?

It is a hand.

What is it?

It is a nose.

What is it?

It is an ear.

Write.

1.

What is it?
It is a mouth.

2.

What is it?
It is an arm.

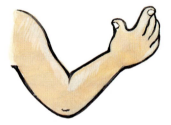

3.

What is it?
It is a foot.

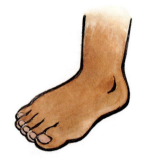

Write and draw.

1.

What is it?
It is an eye.

2.

What
It is a hand.

3.

What

nose.

4.

What

arm.

5.

What

leg.

Plurals

Put -**s** at the end of most plural nouns.

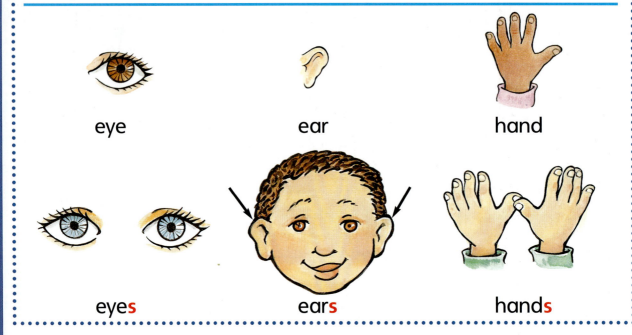

eye

ear

hand

eye**s**

ear**s**

hand**s**

Draw and say.

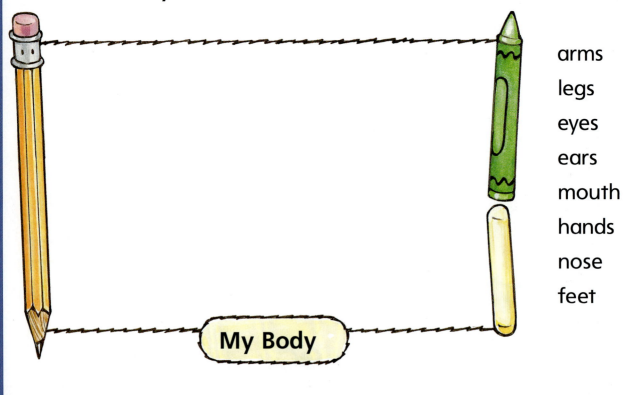

My Body

arms
legs
eyes
ears
mouth
hands
nose
feet

What are they?

What are they?

They are arms.

What are they?

They are eyes.

What are they?

They are hands.

What are they?

They are legs.

Write.

1.

What are they?

They are ears.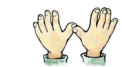

2.

What   ?

They are hands.

3. What are they?

They are legs.

4. What are they?

They are feet.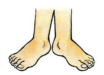

Write and match.

1.

What are they?
They are legs.

2.

What is it?
It _____ mouth.

3.

What are _____ ?

_____ eyes.

4.

What _____ it?

_____ nose.

5.

What _____ ?

_____ ears.

Chant.

What is it?
It's a nose.
It's a nose.
It's a nose.

What is it?
It's a mouth.
It's a mouth.
It's a mouth.

What are they?
They're ears.
They're ears.
They're ears.

What are they?
They're hands.
They're hands.
They're hands.

They're = They are
It's = It is

Color.

Clothes

sweater

coat

pants

shirt

dress

hat

skirt

shoe

sock

This/That

This is a sweater.    That is a sweater.

This is a hat.    That is a hat.

Write.

1.

This is a skirt.

2.

That is a skirt.

3.

This is a dress.

4.

That is a dress.

These/Those

 **These** are shoes.

 **Those** are shoes.

 **These** are socks.

 **Those** are socks.

Write.

1.

These are pants.

2.

Those are hats.

3.

These are coats.

4.

Those are shirts.

Look and circle.

1. (This)/ **That** is a dress.

2. **This** / **That** is a sweater.

3. **These** / **Those** are shoes.

4. **These** / **Those** are socks.

5. **This** / **These** is a skirt.

6. **That** / **Those** are hats.

Adjectives

Adjectives describe nouns.

Size

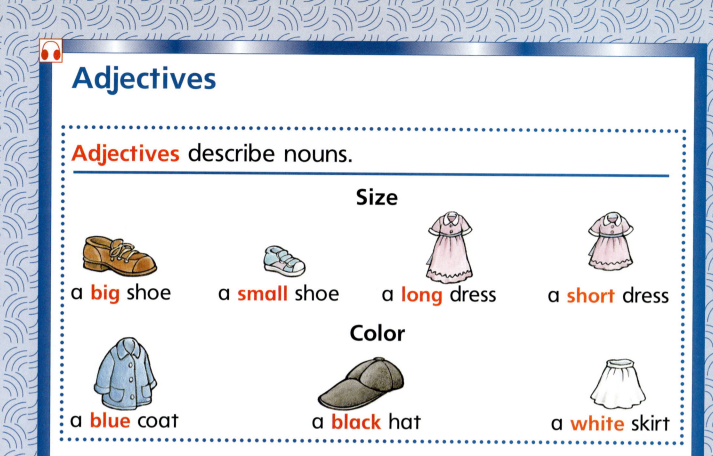

a **big** shoe   a **small** shoe   a **long** dress   a **short** dress

Color

a **blue** coat   a **black** hat   a **white** skirt

Draw, color, and say.

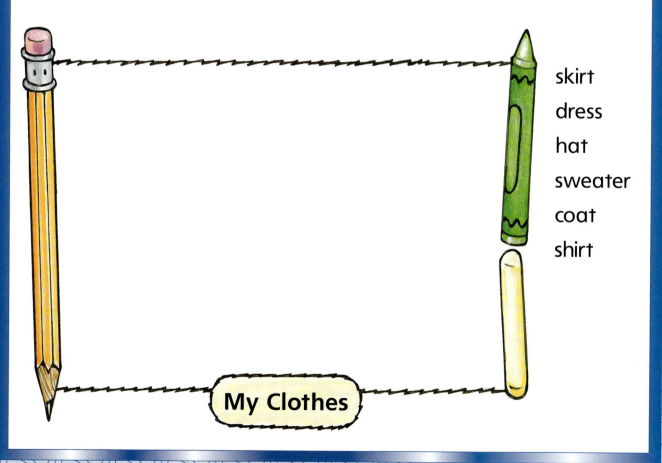

skirt

dress

hat

sweater

coat

shirt

My Clothes

A. Check

1. ☑ This is a big dress.

   ☐ This is a small dress.

2. ☐ This is a long sweater.

   ☐ This is a short sweater.

3. ☐ This is a long skirt.

   ☐ This is a big skirt.

B. Write and color.

1. This is a blue coat.

2. This is a red .

3. yellow .

4. green

🎧 **Chant.**

What's this?
It's a sweater.
What's that?
It's a dress.

What's this?
It's a shirt.
What's that?
It's a hat.

What are those?
They're socks.
What are those?
They're shoes.

what's = what is
it's = it is
they're = they are

Match and color.

Review: Units 3 and 4

Vocabulary

🎧 A. Listen and check.

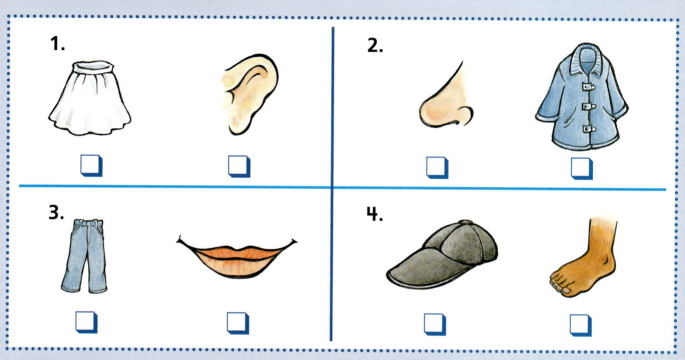

Plurals

🎧 B. Listen and check.

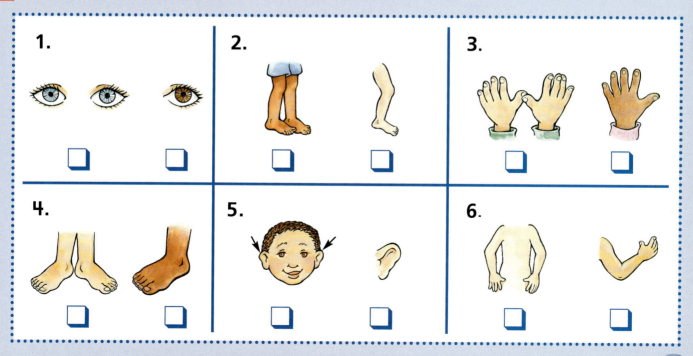

Review: Units 3 and 4

Adjectives

🎧 C. Listen and color.

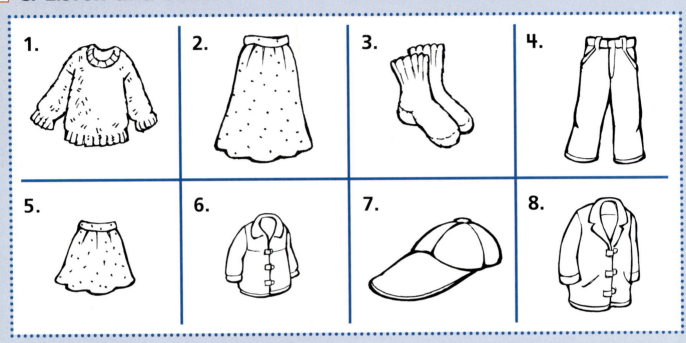

This/That, These/Those

🎧 D. Listen, point, and say.

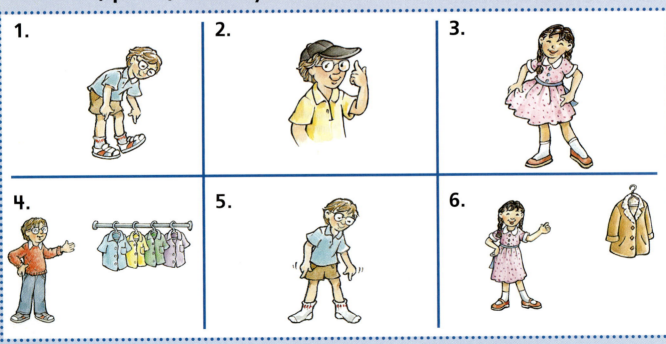

My House

box

bedroom

bathroom

clock

tub

bed

lamp

kitchen

picture

living room

chair

table

In, On, Under

Prepositions describe where a person or thing is.

The clock is **on** the box.

The clock is **in** the box.

The clock is **under** the box.

Write and match.

1. The lamp is ___on___ the table.

2. The clock is ___in___ the tub.

3. The picture is ___under___ the chair.

Where ...?

Where is the clock?

It is on the table.

Where is the lamp?

It is in the box.

Write and match.

1.

Where is the clock?
It is in the tub.

2.

_____ is the picture?
It is _____ the table.

3.

_____ the lamp?
_____ the bed.

A. Circle.

1. The lamp is in / (on) / under the chair.

2. The clock is in / on / under the box.

3. The clock is in / on / under the box.

4. The picture is in / on / under the table.

B. Write.

1. Where is the lamp?

It is _____ the table.

2. Where is the clock?

It is _____ .

3. Where is the picture?

It is _____ .

Present Progressive

The **present progressive** is used to show that an action is happening now.

He **is eating.**

They **are sleeping.**

She **is reading.**

They **are watching** TV.

Write.

1.

He is watching TV.

2.

They are _____.

3.

She is _____.

A. Find and circle.

reading   eating   sleeping   watching

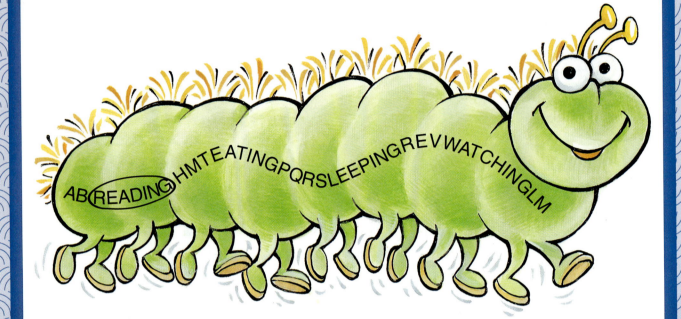

AB READING HMTEATINGPQRSLEEPINGREVWATCHINGLM

B. Write.

1.

She is _____.

2.

They are _____.

3.

He is _____.

4.

She is _____.

He's in the living room.
He's reading.
He's reading.

They're in the living room.
They're reading.
They're reading.

She's in the bedroom.
She's sleeping.
She's sleeping.

They're in the bedroom.
They're sleeping.
They're sleeping.

they're = they are

Find and color.

table   chair   tub   clock   lamp   bed   picture   box

Pets

cat

snake

bird

rabbit

frog

fish

turtle

mouse

Is it a ...?

Is it a mouse?

Yes, it is.

Is it a cat?

No, it isn't.

isn't = is not

Write.

1.

Is it a bird?
Yes, it is.

2.

Is it a cat?
No, it isn't.

3.

_____ rabbit?

Do you have ...?

Draw and say.

A Pet

A. Write the questions.

1.

Do you have a rabbit?

Yes, I do.   (rabbit)

2.

No, I don't.   (turtle)

3.

Yes, I do.   (mouse)

B. Write the answers.

1. Do you have a snake?

No, I don't.

2. Do you have a cat?

Yes, I   .

3. Do you have a bird?

What does he/she have?

What does he have?

He has a rabbit.

What does she have?

She has a frog.

Write.

1.

What does he have?
He has a fish.

2.

What does she have?
She has a _____ .

3.

What _____ ?
He has a _____ .

A. Write the answers.

1. What does he have?

He has a mouse.

2. What does she have?

3. What does he have?

B. Write the questions.

1.

What does she have?

She has a turtle.

2.

He has a snake.

3.

She has a rabbit.

🎧 **Chant.**

What does she have?
Is it a cat?
Yes, it is.
Yes, it is.

What does she have?
Is it a snake?
Yes, it is.
Yes, it is.

What does she have?
Is it a frog?
Yes, it is.
Yes, it is.

What is it?

1.

It is a cat.

2.

3.

4.

5.

6.

7.

8.

Review: Units 5 and 6

Vocabulary

🎧 A. Listen and check.

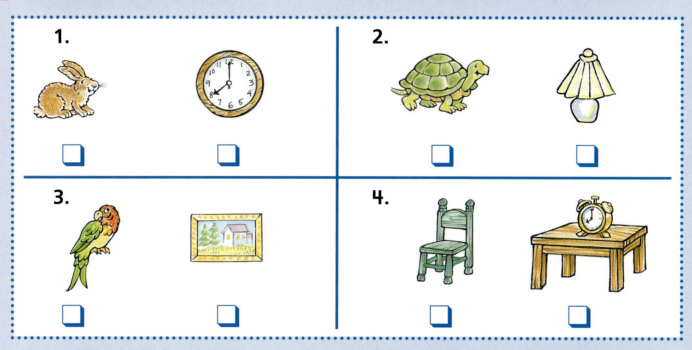

1.
2.
3.
4.

In, On, Under

🎧 B. Listen and check.

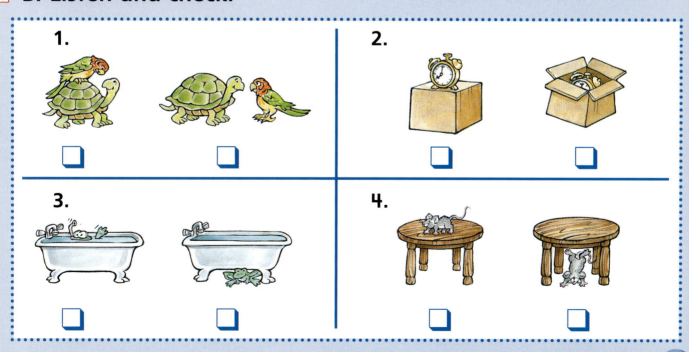

1.
2.
3.
4.

Review: Units 5 and 6

Have

🎧 C. Listen and check.

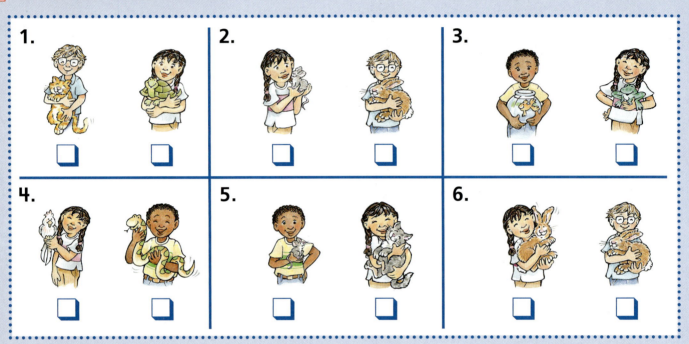

Present Progressive

🎧 D. Listen, point, and say.

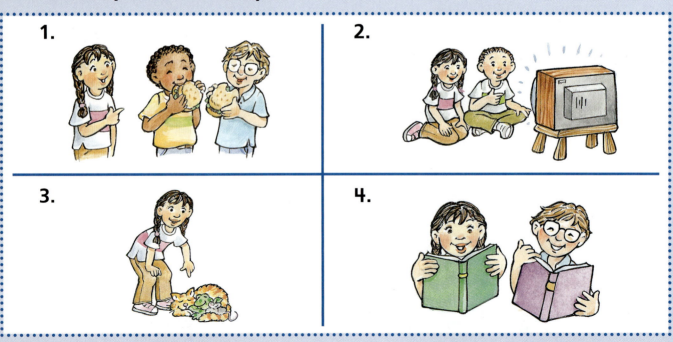

Happy Birthday!

balloon

camera

candle

cake

card

ice cream

candy

present

game

How old ...?

How old are you?   I'm 6 years old.

I'm = I am

A. Write the questions.

1.

How old are you?
I'm 6 years old.

2.

I'm 5 years old.

3.

I'm 7 years old.

B. Write the answer.
How old are you?

His/Her

His and her show belonging.

This is **her** present.

This is **his** balloon.

Circle.

1. This is (**his**)/ **her** cake.

2. This is **his** / **her** camera.

3. This is **his** / **her** candy.

4. This is **his** / **her** ice cream.

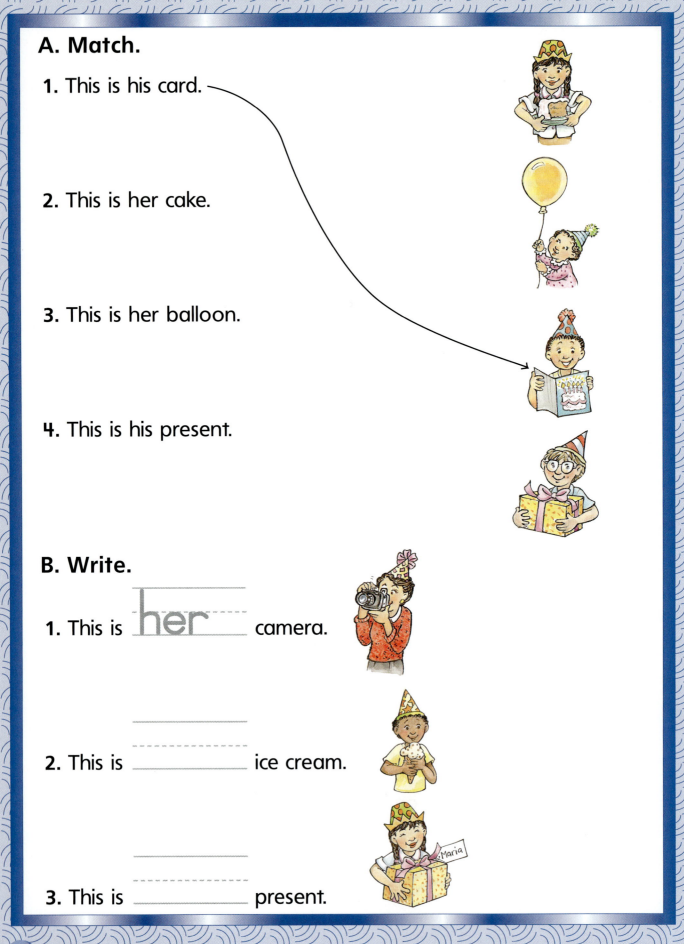

A. Match.

1. This is his card.

2. This is her cake.

3. This is her balloon.

4. This is his present.

B. Write.

1. This is her camera.

2. This is _____ ice cream.

3. This is _____ present.

Whose ...?

Whose present is this?

It's her present.

It's = It is

Write the question.

1.

Whose ice cream is this?

It's her ice cream.

2.

It's his card.

3.

It's her camera.

4.

It's his balloon.

Write.

1. Whose candy is this?

It's her candy.

2. Whose present is this?

 his present.

3. Whose balloon is this?

4. Whose ice cream _____ this?

5. Whose card is _____ ?

It's my birthday.
I'm 6.
I'm 6.

It's her birthday.
She's 10.
She's 10.

It's his birthday.
He's 8.
He's 8.

It's = It is
I'm = I am
She's = She is
He's = He is

Match and color.

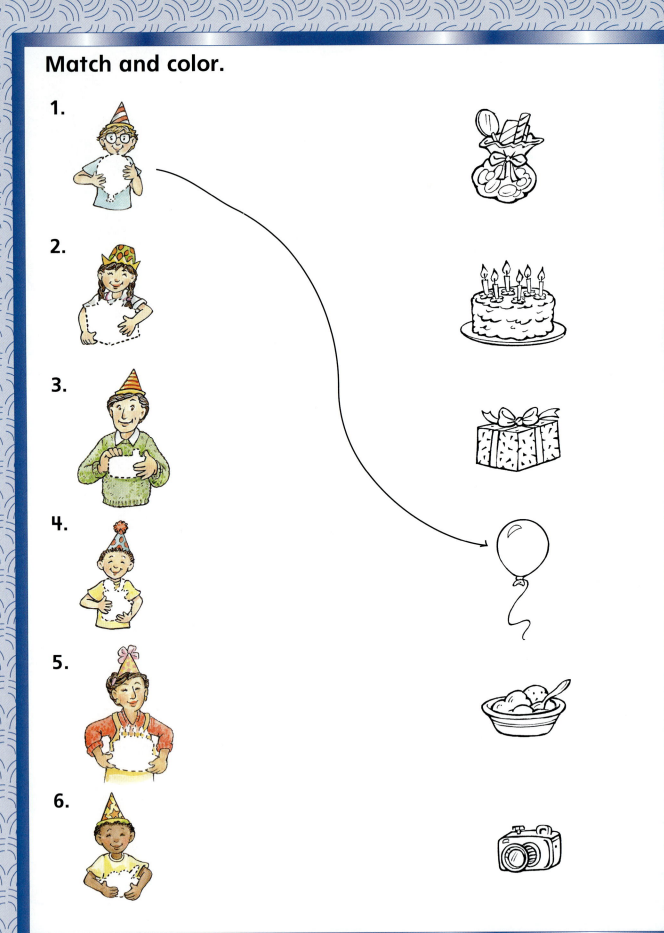

1.

2.

3.

4.

5.

6.

In the Toy Store

kite

train

doll

yo-yo

car

crayon

ball

puzzle

boat

Does he/she like ...?

Does he like cars?

Yes, he does.

Does she like yo-yos?

No, she doesn't.

Write.

1.

Does he like yo-yos?

No, he doesn't.

2.

dolls?

Yes, she does.

3.

kites?

No, he doesn't.

4.

crayons?

Yes, she does.

A. Write the answers.

1. Does he like boats?

Yes, he does.

2. Does she like cars?

_____

_____

3. Does he like dolls?

_____

_____

4. Does she like kites?

_____

_____

B. Write the questions.

1.

Does he like trains?

Yes, he does.   (trains)

2.

_____

_____

Yes, he does.   (crayons)

3.

_____

_____

No, she doesn't.   (balls)

Do you like ...?

Do you like dolls?

Yes, I do.

Do you like puzzles?

No, I don't.

Write and check.

1.

Do you like crayons?

❏ Yes, I do.
❏ No, I don't.

2.

puzzles?

❏ Yes, I do.
❏ No, I don't.

3.

yo-yos?

❏ Yes, I do.
❏ No, I don't.

4.

dolls?

❏ Yes, I do.
❏ No, I don't.

Do you want ...?

Do you want a yo-yo?

Yes, I do.

Do you want a yo-yo?

No, I don't.
I want a kite.

Draw and write.

I want a _____

Write.

1.

Do you **want** a puzzle?

Yes, I do.

2.

Do you _____ a doll?

No, _____

3.

Do you _____ a car?

_____

Chant.

Do you want,
Do you want,
Do you want a train?

Yes, yes,
Yes, I do.
Yes, I want a train!

Do you want,
Do you want,
Do you want a ball?

Yes, yes,
Yes, I do.
Yes, I want a ball.

Do you like ...?

Drop a paper clip onto an object in the circle.

Review: Units 7 and 8

Vocabulary

🎧 **A. Listen and check.**

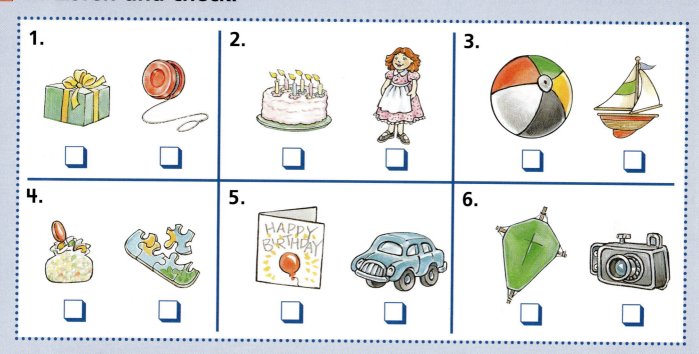

His/Her

🎧 **B. Listen and check.**

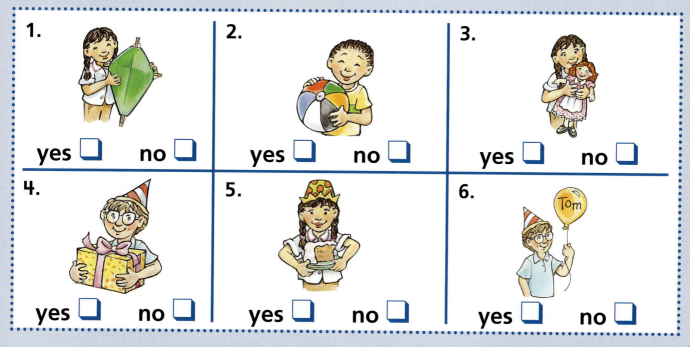

Review: Units 7 and 8

Does he/she like ...?

C. Listen and check.

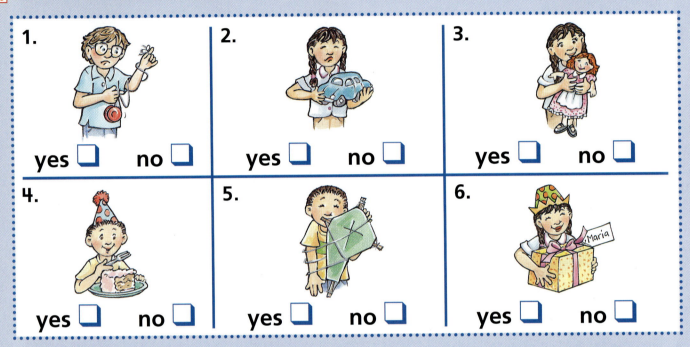

1. yes ☐   no ☐
2. yes ☐   no ☐
3. yes ☐   no ☐
4. yes ☐   no ☐
5. yes ☐   no ☐
6. yes ☐   no ☐

Do you like ...?

D. Listen, point, and say.

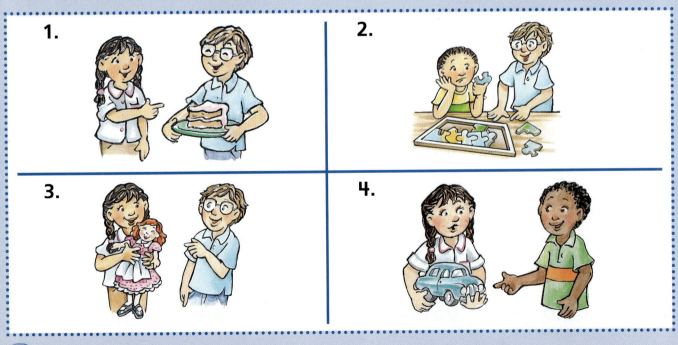

1.
2.
3.
4.

Outdoor Activities

fly a kite

climb a tree

play soccer

run

jump

swim

ride a bike

Can

Use **can** to show ability.

I **can** run.

I **can** swim.

He **can** run.

She **can** swim.

Write.

1.

She can run.

2.

He can

3.

She

4.

He

Can't

I **can't** jump.

I **can't** play soccer.

He **can't** ride a bike.

She **can't** fly a kite.

can't = can not

Write.

1.

He can't play soccer.

2.

She can't _____ .

3.

4.

Look at the chart and write.

Sam	yes	no	yes	no
Tom	yes	no	yes	yes
Maria	yes	yes	no	no

1. Maria <u>can</u> ride <u>a bike.</u>

2. Sam <u>can't</u> climb <u>a tree.</u>

3. Tom _____ ride <u>a bike.</u>

4. Maria _____ fly <u>a kite.</u>

5. Tom _____ play <u>soccer.</u>

6. Sam _____ fly <u>a kite.</u>

Can you ...?

Can you swim?

Yes, I can.

Write and check.

1.

Can you run?

❏ Yes, I can.
❏ No, I can't.

2.

Can you swim?

❏ Yes, I can.
❏ No, I can't.

3.

Can you play soccer?

❏ Yes, I can.
❏ No, I can't.

4.

Can you fly a kite?

❏ Yes, I can.
❏ No, I can't.

Can he/she ...?

Can he fly a kite?

Yes, he can.

Can she play soccer?

No, she can't.

Write the questions.

1.

Can he _____?

Yes, he can.

2.

_____

No, she can't.

3.

_____

Yes, she can.

4.

_____

No, he can't.

Can you run?

Yes, I can.

Yes, I can.

Can you swim?

Yes, I can.

Yes, I can.

Can you jump?

Yes, I can.

Yes, I can.

Draw 2 things you can do. Then write.

1.

I can _____.

2.

I can _____.

Food

cookies
bananas
hot dog
cake
grapes
drink
milk
juice
hamburger

What are you doing?

What are you doing?

I am baking cookies.

Write the questions.

1.

What are you doing?

I am washing the dishes.

2.

I am eating a hot dog.

3.

I am drinking milk.

4.

I am baking a cake.

What is he/she doing?

What is he doing?

He is baking a cake.

What is she doing?

She is drinking juice.

Write.

1.

What is she doing?

She is washing the dishes.
(wash)

2.

What ?

He is cookies.
(eat)

3.

What ?

She is milk.
(drink)

A. Write sentences.

1. (He / eat / a hot dog)

He is eating a hot dog.

2. (She / drink / juice)

3. (I / bake / cookies)

B. Write the questions.

1.

What are you doing?

I am washing the dishes.

2.

He is eating a hamburger.

3.

She is baking cookies.

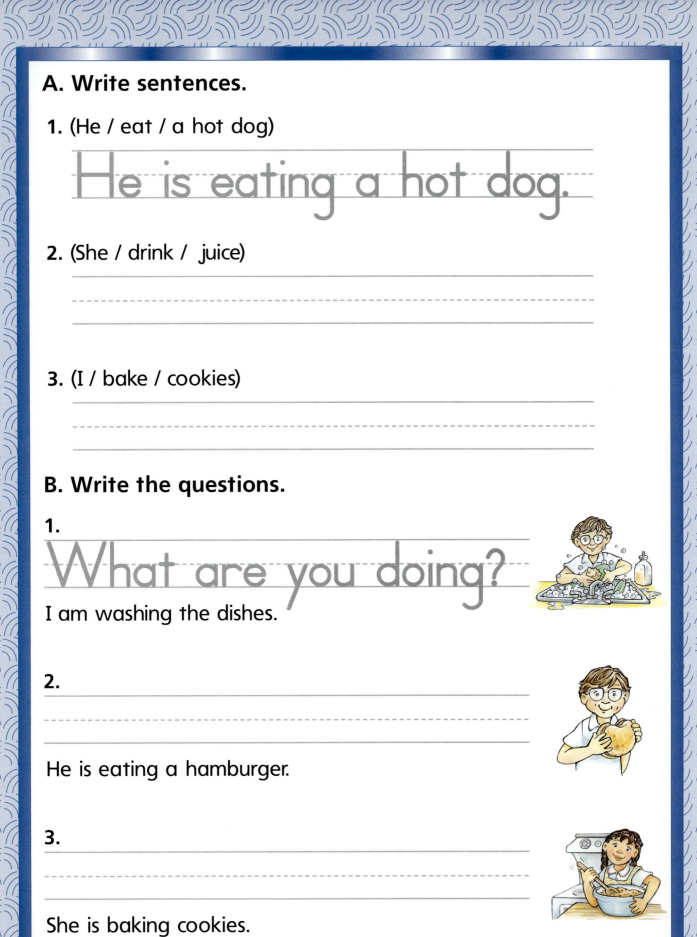

How many . . .?

How many hamburgers do you want?

I want 2 hamburgers.

Write.

1.

How many hot dogs do you want?

I want 3 hot dogs.

2.

bananas do you want?

I want 4 bananas.

3.

grapes do you want?

I want 13 grapes.

4.

cookies do you want?

I want 10 cookies.

Write the answers and draw.

1. How many hamburgers do you want?

I want 5 hamburgers.

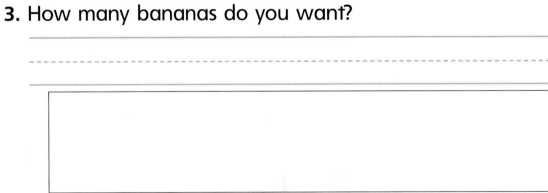

2. How many grapes do you want?

3. How many bananas do you want?

4. How many cookies do you want?

What are you doing?
What are you doing?

I am eating bananas.
I am eating bananas.

What are you doing?
What are you doing?

I am eating hamburgers.
I am eating hamburgers.

What are you doing?
What are you doing?

I am eating grapes.
I am eating grapes.

Find and color.

2 bananas   3 cookies   1 hot dog   2 cakes

Review: Units 9 and 10

Vocabulary

🎧 **A. Listen and check.**

Can/Can't

🎧 **B. Listen and check.**

Review: Units 9 and 10

Present Progressive

🎧 **C. Listen and check.**

1. yes ☐ no ☐

2. yes ☐ no ☐

3. yes ☐ no ☐

4. yes ☐ no ☐

How many ...?

🎧 **D. Listen, point, and say.**

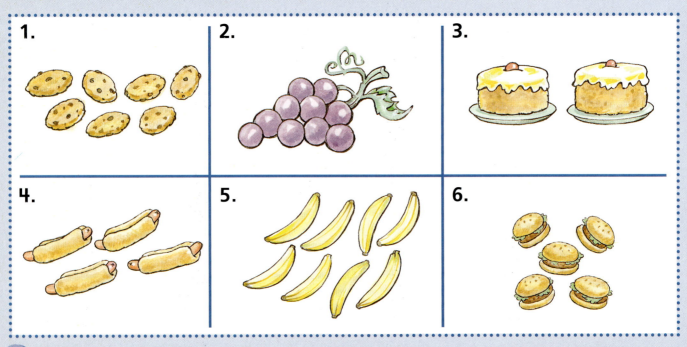

1.

2.

3.

4.

5.

6.

Alphabet Practice

A a B b C c

D d E e F f

G g H h I i

J j K k L l

M m N n O o

P p Q q R r

S s T t U u

V v W w X x

Y y Z z

Number Practice

1   2

3   4

5   6

7   8

9   10

11   12

13   14

15   16

17   18

19   20

Ii

Ee

Aa

Jj

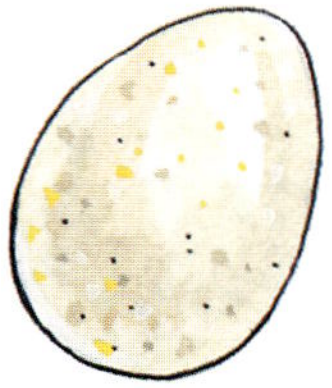

Ff

Bb

Kk

Gg

Cc

Ll

Hh

Dd

Mm

V v

R r

N n

W w

S s

O o

X x

T t

P p

Y y

U u

Q q

Z z

Word List

apple

arm

bake

ball

balloon

banana

bathroom

bed

bedroom

bird

boat

book

box

brother

cake

camera

candle

candy

car

card

cat

chair

classroom

climb

clock

coat

cookie

crayon

desk

doll

dress

drink

ear

eat

eye

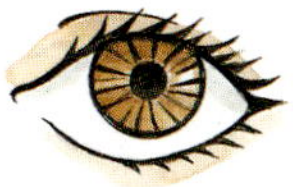

father

feet

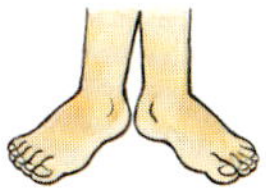

fish

fly

foot

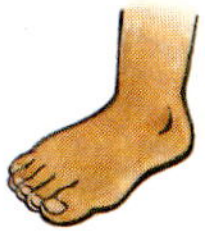

frog

game

grandfather

grandmother

grapes

hamburger

hand

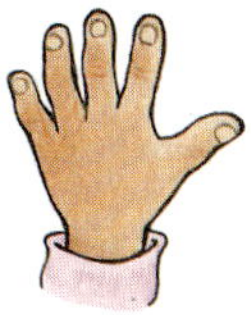

hat

hot dog

living room

ice cream

milk

juice

mother

jump

mouse

kitchen

mouth

kite

nose

lamp

pants

leg

pencil

picture		shirt	
play		shoe	
present		sister	
puzzle		skirt	
rabbit		sleep	
read		snake	
ride		sock	
run		student	

sweater

swim

table

teacher

train

tub

turtle

umbrella

wash

watch

yo-yo